Notice everything.

Appreciate everything,

including the ordinary.

That's how to click in with

joyfulness or cheerfulness.

Curiosity encourages cheering up.

So does simply remembering

to do something different.

Living Beautifully

AN INSPIRATIONAL JOURNAL

PEMA CHÖDRÖN

SHAMBHALA

BOULDER

Shambhala Publications, Inc.
4720 Walnut Street
Boulder, Colorado 80301
shambhala.com

The material in this book is derived from the following previously published Shambhala Publications books: *Living Beautifully with Uncertainty and Change*, *Welcoming the Unwelcome*, *When Things Fall Apart*, *Start Where You Are*, and *The Wisdom of No Escape*.

9 8 7 6 5 4 3 2 1

First Edition

Printed in the United States of America

⊗ This edition is printed on acid-free paper that meets the American National Standards Institute Z39.48 Standard.

♻ Shambhala makes every effort to print on recycled paper. For more information please visit www.shambhala.com.

Shambhala Publications is distributed worldwide by Penguin Random House, Inc., and its subsidiaries.

Cover illustrations by Jasmine Dowling
Cover art by Vadim Georgiev/Shutterstock
Cover and interior design by Shubhani Sarkar

Library of Congress Cataloging-in-Publication Data

Names: Chödrön, Pema, author.
Title: Living beautifully: an inspirational journal.
Description: First edition. | Boulder: Shambhala, 2019.
Identifiers: LCCN 2019022809 | ISBN 9781611808056 (paperback)
Subjects: LCSH: Chödrön, Pema—Quotations. | Spiritual life—Buddhism. |
Compassion—Religious aspects—Buddhism. | Spiritual journals.
Classification: LCC BQ5660 .C485 2019 | DDC 294.3/4432—dc23
LC record available at https://lccn.loc.gov/2019022809

Welcome.

YOU ALREADY HAVE EVERYTHING YOU NEED. THERE IS NO NEED for self-improvement. All these trips that we lay on ourselves—the heavy-duty fearing that we're bad and hoping that we're good, the identities that we so dearly cling to, the rage, the jealousy, and the addictions of all kinds—never touch our basic wealth. They are like clouds that temporarily block the sun. But all the time our warmth and brilliance are right here. This is who we really are. We are one blink of an eye away from being fully awake.

Looking at ourselves this way is very different from our usual habit. From this perspective we don't need to change: you can feel as wretched as you like, and you're still a good candidate for enlightenment. You can feel like the world's most hopeless basket case, but that feeling is your wealth, not something to be thrown out or improved upon. There's a richness to all of the smelly stuff that we so dislike and so little desire. The delightful things—what we love so dearly about ourselves, the places in which we feel some sense of pride or inspiration—these also are our wealth.

With this journal, you can start just where you are. If you're feeling angry, poverty-stricken, or depressed, I hope this journal will encourage you to use all the unwanted things in your life as the means for awakening compassion for yourself and others.

Pema Chödrön

Impermanence Practice

WHEN IMPERMANENCE PRESENTS ITSELF IN OUR LIVES, WE CAN recognize it as impermanence. We don't have to look for opportunities to do this. When your pen runs out of ink in the middle of writing an important letter, recognize it as impermanence, part of the whole cycle of life. When someone's born, recognize it as impermanence. When someone dies, recognize it as impermanence. When your car gets stolen, recognize it as impermanence. When you fall in love, recognize it as impermanence, and let that intensify the preciousness. When a relationship ends, recognize it as impermanence. There are countless examples of impermanence in our lives every day, from the moment we wake up until we fall asleep and even while we're dreaming, all the time. This is a twenty-four-hour-a-day practice. Recognize impermanence as impermanence.

Then we can recognize our reaction to impermanence. This is where curiosity comes in. Usually we just react habitually to events in our lives. We become resentful or delighted, excited or disappointed. There's no intelligence involved, no cheerfulness. But when we recognize impermanence as impermanence, we can also notice what our reaction to impermanence is. This is called mindfulness, awareness, curiosity, inquisitiveness, paying attention. Whatever we call it, it's a very helpful practice, the practice of coming to know ourselves completely.

Acknowledging the preciousness of each day is a good way to live, a good way to reconnect with our basic joy.

Rather than being disheartened by the ambiguity, the uncertainty of life, what if we accepted it and relaxed into it? What if we said, "Yes, this is the way it is; this is what it means to be human," and decided to sit down and enjoy the ride?

Joy has to do with seeing

how big, how completely

unobstructed, and how

precious things are.

Although it is embarrassing
and painful, it is very healing
to stop hiding from yourself. It
is healing to know all the ways
that you're sneaky, all the ways
that you hide out, all the ways
that you shut down, deny, close
off, criticize people,

all your weird little ways. You can know all that with some sense of humor and kindness. By knowing yourself, you're coming to know humanness altogether. We are all up against these things. We are all in this together.

When you realize that you're talking to yourself,

label it "thinking" and notice your tone of voice.

Let it be compassionate and gentle and humorous.

Then you'll be changing old stuck patterns that are

shared by the whole human race. Compassion for

others begins with kindness to ourselves.

Every day, at the moment when things get edgy, we can just ask ourselves, "Am I going to practice peace, or am I going to war?"

Fear is a natural reaction to

moving closer to the truth.

When we protect ourselves so we won't feel pain,

that protection becomes like armor, like armor that

imprisons the softness of the heart.

The on-the-spot practice of being

fully present, feeling your heart, and

greeting the next moment with an

open mind can be done at any time:

when you wake up in the morning,

before a difficult conversation,

whenever fear or discomfort arises.

This practice is a beautiful way to

claim your warriorship, your spiritual

warriorship. In other words, it is a way

to claim your courage, your kindness,

your strength.

You build inner strength

through embracing the

totality of your experience,

both the delightful parts

and the difficult parts.

At some point, if you're fortunate, you'll hit a wall of truth and wonder what you've been doing with your life. At that point you'll feel highly motivated to find out what frees you and helps you to be kinder and more loving, less affliction driven and confused.

The pain of the world pierces

us to the heart, but we

never forget the goodness

of being alive.

We can dance with life when it's a wild party completely out of control, and we can dance with life when it's as tender as a lover. We work with whatever we have, with whoever we are, right now.

Only by learning to fully

embrace all aspects of

ourselves—even the most

seemingly negative elements of

our minds and hearts—will we

learn to fully embrace others.

Only by discovering the basic

goodness in both our lotus and

our mud will we come to see the

basic goodness of all living beings.

The time we live in

is a fertile ground for

training in being

open-minded and

open-hearted.

Life doesn't have to be one way or the other. We don't have to jump back and forth. We can live beautifully with whatever comes—heartache and joy, success and failure, instability and change.

May we all learn that pain is not the end of the journey, and neither is delight. We can hold them both—indeed hold it all—at the same time, remembering that everything in these quixotic,

unpredictable, unsettled and

unsettling, exhilarating and

heart-stirring times is a doorway

to awakening in a sacred world.

Be fully present.

Feel your heart.

Engage the next moment

without an agenda.

Our aim is to fully awaken our heart and mind, not just for our own greater well-being, but to bring benefit, solace, and wisdom to other living beings. What motivation could top that?

Thoughts go through our minds all the time, and when we sit, we are providing a lot of space for all of them to arise. Like clouds in a big sky or waves in a vast sea, all our thoughts are given the space to appear. If one hangs on and sweeps us away, whether we call it pleasant or unpleasant, the instruction is to label it all "thinking" with as much openness and kindness as we can muster and let it dissolve back into the big sky. When the clouds and waves immediately return, it's no problem. We just acknowledge them again and again with unconditional friendliness, labeling them as just "thinking" and letting them go again and again and again. If we can go beyond blame and other escapes and just feel the bleeding, raw meat quality of our vulnerability, we can enter a space where the best part of us comes out.

The wonderful irony about this spiritual journey is that

we find it only leads us to become just as we are.

The exalted state of enlightenment is nothing

more than fully knowing ourselves and

our world, just as we are.

Most of us are a rich mixture of rough and smooth, bitter and sweet. But wherever we are right now, whatever our lives are like in the moment, this is our mandala, our working basis for awakening.

To be fully alive, fully human,

and completely awake is to be

continually thrown out of the

nest. To live fully is to be always

in no-man's-land, to experience

each moment as completely

new and fresh. To live is to be

willing to die over and over

again. From the awakened

point of view, that's life.

The more willing you are to step out of your comfort
zone, the more comfortable you feel in your life.
Situations that used to arouse fear and nausea
become easier to relax in. On the other hand,
if you stay in the comfort zone
all the time, it shrinks.

Never underestimate the power of mind. How you work with things really can transform what seems to be. Working with the inner has the ability to transform the outer—though not in any linear way you can put your finger on.

Practicing open awareness is a gradual process of

continually going back to seeing what

we're seeing, smelling what we're smelling,

feeling what we're feeling.

We can get used to the fleeting quality

of life in a natural, gentle, even joyful

way, by watching the seasons change,

watching day turn to night,

watching children grow up,

watching sand castles dissolve back

into the sea. But if we don't find

some way to make friends

with groundlessness and the

ever-changing energy of life, then

we'll always be struggling to find

stability in a shifting world.

Whenever we are between here and there, whenever one

thing has ended and we're waiting for the next thing

to begin, whenever we're tempted to distract ourselves

or look for an escape route, we can instead let ourselves

be open, curious, tentative, vulnerable.

The next time you encounter
fear, consider yourself lucky.
This is where the courage
comes in. Usually we think that
brave people have no fear.
The truth is that they are
intimate with fear.

Letting there be room for not knowing is the most important thing of all. We try to do what we think is going to help. But we don't know. We never know if we're going to fall flat or sit up tall. When there's

a big disappointment,

we don't know if that's the

end of the story. It may be just

the beginning of a

great adventure.

We don't sit in meditation to become good meditators. We sit in meditation so that we'll be more awake in our lives.

Everything that occurs is not only usable and workable but is actually the path itself. We can use everything that happens to us as the means for waking up.

The most difficult times for many of us are the ones we give ourselves.

Feelings like disappointment, embarrassment, irritation, resentment, anger, jealousy, and fear, instead of being bad news, are actually very clear moments that teach us where it is that we're holding back. They teach us to perk up and lean in when we feel we'd rather collapse and

walk away. They're like messengers

that show us, with terrifying clarity,

exactly where we're stuck.

This very moment is the perfect

teacher, and, lucky for us, it's

with us wherever we are.

Rather than letting our negativity get the better of us,
we could acknowledge that right now we feel like a
piece of shit and not be squeamish about taking a
good look. That's the compassionate thing to do.
That's the brave thing to do.

Who are the people you really dislike and wish would simply go away? Who's on your list? Be grateful to them: they're your own special gurus, showing up right on time to keep you honest.

To the degree that we have compassion for ourselves, we will also have compassion for others. Having compassion starts and ends with having compassion for all those unwanted parts of ourselves, all those imperfections that we don't even want to look at.

What we call obstacles are really the way the world and our entire experience teach us where we're stuck. What may appear to be an arrow or a sword we can actually experience as a flower. Whether we experience what happens

to us as obstacle and enemy or

as teacher and friend depends

entirely on our perception

of reality. It depends on our

relationship with ourselves.

When we begin just to try to accept ourselves,

the ancient burden of self-importance lightens

up considerably. Finally there's room for genuine

inquisitiveness, and we find we have an appetite

for what's out there.

The time is now, not later.

This is our choice in every moment. Do we relate to our circumstances with bitterness or with openness?

Every act counts. Every thought and emotion counts too. This is all the path we have. This is where we apply the teachings. This is where we come to understand why we meditate.

We are only going to be here for a short while. Even if we live to be 108, our life will be too short for witnessing all its wonders. The dharma is each act, each thought, each word we speak.

When our bubble bursts, we can recognize that we are walking through a very important doorway. Then we can experiment with hanging out on the other side of that doorway. We can learn to relax there.

Don't worry about achieving.

Don't worry about perfection.

Just be there each moment as

best you can.

Life is a good teacher and a good friend. Things are always in transition, if we could only realize it. Nothing ever sums itself up in the way that we like to dream about.

The off-center, in-between state

is an ideal situation, a situation

in which we don't get caught and

we can open our hearts and

minds beyond limit.

Learning how to be kind to ourselves, learning how to respect ourselves, is important. The reason it's important is that, fundamentally, when we look into our own hearts and begin to discover what is confused and what is brilliant, what is bitter and what is sweet, it isn't just ourselves that we're discovering. We're discovering the universe.

Meditation practice isn't about trying to throw ourselves away and become something better. It's about befriending who we are already.

What you do for yourself—

any gesture of kindness, any

gesture of gentleness, any

gesture of honesty and clear

seeing toward yourself—will

affect how you experience your

world. In fact, it will transform

how you experience the world.

What you do for yourself,

you're doing for others, and

what you do for others, you're

doing for yourself.

We don't get wise by staying in

a room with all the doors

and windows closed.

Whatever you're given can wake you up or put you to sleep. That's the challenge of now: What are you going to do with what you have already—your body, your speech, your mind?

Well-being of mind is like a mountain lake without ripples. When the lake has no ripples, everything in the lake can be seen. When the water is all churned up, nothing can be seen. The still lake without ripples is an image of our minds

at ease, so full of unlimited

friendliness for all the junk

at the bottom of the lake that

we don't feel the need to churn

up the waters just to avoid

looking at what's there.

Gloriousness and wretchedness need each other. One inspires us, the other softens us. They go together.

Whether we consider what happens to us good fortune
or ill fortune, appreciation for this life can wake us
up and give us the courage we need to stay right
there with whatever comes through the door.

Whether we're conscious of

it or not, the ground is always

shifting. Nothing lasts,

including us.

It's up to you how to use your life.

Maybe the most important

teaching is to lighten up

and relax.

The path is uncharted. It comes into existence

moment by moment and at the same time

drops away behind us.

Photograph by Christine Alicino

About the Author

ANI PEMA CHÖDRÖN was born Deirdre Blomfield-Brown in 1936, in New York City. She attended Miss Porter's School in Connecticut and graduated from the University of California at Berkeley. She taught elementary school for many years in both New Mexico and California. Pema has two children and three grandchildren.

While in her mid-thirties, Ani Pema traveled to the French Alps and encountered Lama Chime Rinpoche, with whom she studied for several years. She became a novice nun in 1974 while studying with Lama Chime in London. His Holiness the Sixteenth Karmapa came to Scotland at that time, and Ani Pema received her ordination from him.

Ani Pema first met her root guru, Chögyam Trungpa Rinpoche, in 1972. Lama Chime encouraged her to work with Rinpoche, and it was with him that she ultimately made her most profound connection, studying with him from 1974 until his death in 1987. At the request of the Sixteenth Karmapa, she received the full bikshuni ordination in the Chinese lineage of Buddhism in 1981 in Hong Kong. She served as the director of Karma Dzong in Boulder, Colorado, until moving in 1984 to rural Cape Breton, Nova Scotia, to be the director of Gampo Abbey. Chögyam Trungpa Rinpoche gave her explicit instructions on establishing this monastery for Western monks and nuns.

Ani Pema currently teaches in the United States and Canada and plans for an increased amount of time in solitary retreat under the guidance of Venerable Dzigar Kongtrul Rinpoche. Her nonprofit, The Pema Chödrön Foundation, was set up to assist in sharing the ideas and teachings of Buddhism in the West.

She is the author of numerous books and audiobooks.

Books by Pema Chödrön